I0893524

AMAZING PLANTS

Annabel Griffin

Illustrated by Tjarda Borsboom

Copyright © 2024 Hungry Tomato Ltd

First published in 2024 by Hungry Tomato Ltd
F15, Old Bakery Studios, Blewetts Wharf, Malpas Road,
Truro, Cornwall, TR1 1QH, UK.

No part of this publication may be reproduced, stored in a retrieval system, or transmitted in any form or by any means, electronic, mechanical, photocopying, recording, or otherwise, without prior written permission of the copyright owner.

A CIP catalog record for this book is available from the British Library.

ISBN 9781835690062

Printed in China

Discover more at
www.hungrytomato.com

Picture Credits:
Abbreviations: m-middle, t-top, l-left, r-right, bg-background.

Shutterstock: Arunee Rodley 18tr; Bryan Faust 20mr; Dendy12 19bm; Guilhermesoares 23ml; Kevin Case 23tl; LEOCHEN66 21ml; Michal Ninger 23br; Natallia Ustsinava 20bl; New Africa 18bl; The Natures 19tl; Vinicius R.Souza 23mr; Wilaiwan Jantra 19tr; Zhukova Valentyna 23tr; Zulazhar 23bl.

Every effort has been made to trace the copyright holders, and we apologize in advance for any unintentional omissions. We would be pleased to insert the appropriate acknowledgments in any subsequent edition of this publication.

Contents

What Is a Plant?	4	Mighty Moss	16
Prehistoric Plants	6	Prize Plants	18
Biggest Plants	8	Did You Know?	20
Smelliest Plants	10	Match Up the Pairs	22
Meat-eating Plants	12	Glossary	24
Is It a Plant?	14		

Words in **BOLD** can be found in the glossary.

What Is a Plant?

Plants are living things that can be found almost everywhere on Earth! There are over 300,000 different types of plants on our planet. How many can you name?

Plants come in all sorts of shapes and sizes, but most of them have the same three parts: stem, roots, and leaves.

Leaves

Leaves are very important. They help the plant make its own food, to give it energy and help it grow.

Stem

A plant's stem grows above the ground and gives support. It acts as a drinking straw for the plant, carrying water and **nutrients** from the roots to different parts of the plant.

Roots

Roots are usually hidden underground. They help to hold the plant in place, like an anchor. They also take up water and nutrients from the soil that the plant needs to grow.

Some plants have other features, such as fruit, flowers, thorns, and branches.

Prehistoric Plants

There have been plants growing on Earth for around 500 million years. Some that were around when dinosaurs roamed the Earth still exist today!

Back when T.rex was stomping around, the world was hotter and wetter than it is today.

Green, leafy plants, like ferns and cycads, were around long before flowering plants started to grow.

Ginkgo trees

Ginkgo trees are **"living fossils"**. They have changed very little in 270 million years.

Horsetails

Horsetails existed millions of years ago. They were probably a tasty snack for plant-eating dinosaurs!

Tree fern

Tree ferns are a type of fern that have tree-like trunks. They grow very slowly, about 1 inch (2.5cm) per year.

Magnolia

Magnolias are one of the oldest known flowering plants. In the times before bees existed, flowers were **pollinated** by prehistoric beetles instead.

Cycad

Cycads and tree ferns aren't related, but look similar. Cycads produce cones full of seeds, whereas tree ferns create **spores.**

Hard fern

Ferns are one of the oldest groups of plants on the planet. If you went back 300 million years, you would find them!

Biggest Plants

The largest trees in the world stretch higher than some skyscrapers, even the Statue of Liberty!

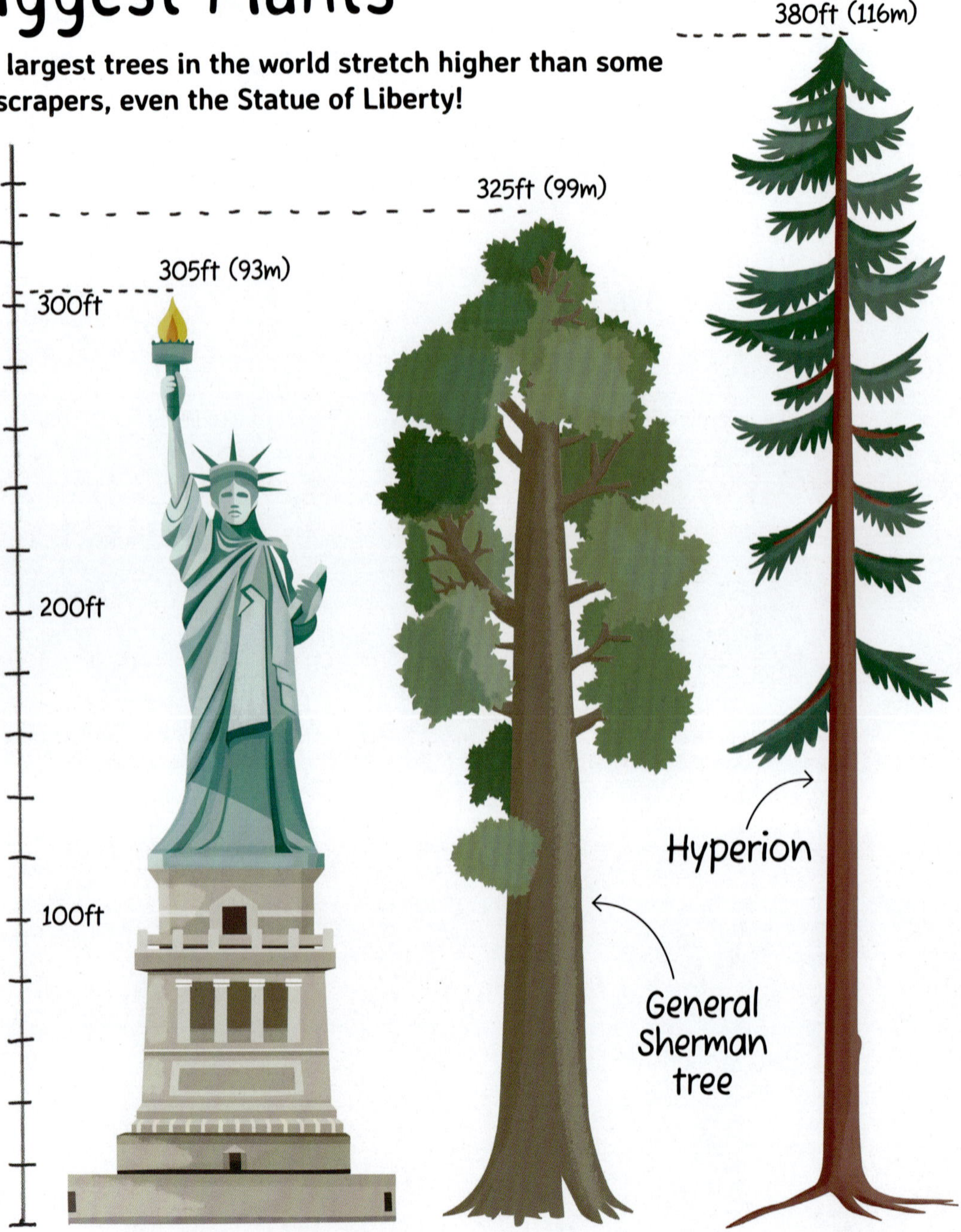

World's largest tree

The General Sherman tree is the largest tree in the world overall. It grows in California, USA, and is thought to be 2,200–2,700 years old.

World's tallest tree

The Hyperion redwood tree in California, USA, measures a mighty 380 feet (116m) in height. It's the tallest tree in the world!

World's widest tree

El Árbol del Tule, in Mexico, is 46 feet (14m) wide. That's wider than the length of a bus!

World's biggest plant

The biggest plant in the world isn't a tree, it's a 4,500-year-old underwater seagrass meadow that has grown from just one **seedling** and spread!

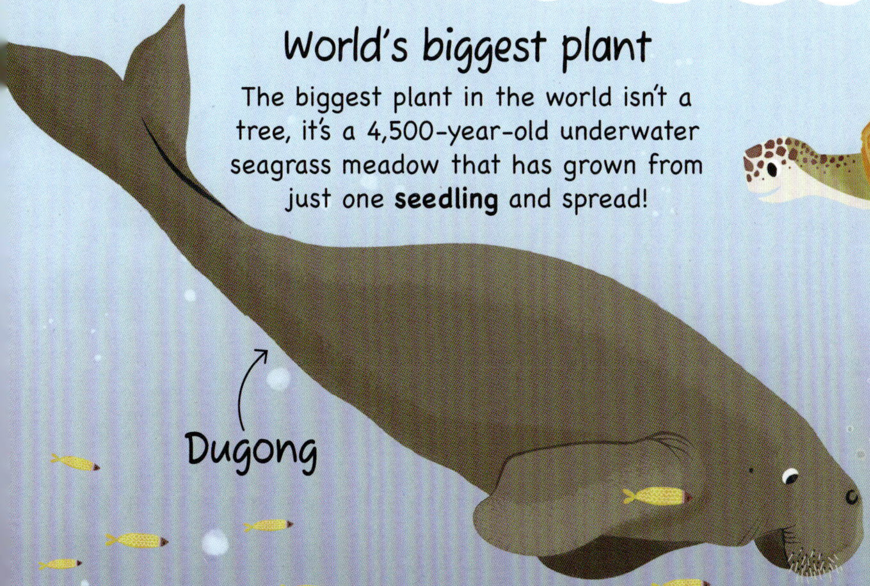

The seagrass banks in Shark Bay, Australia, are the biggest in the world!

Smelliest Plants

Some plants smell good enough to eat, while others might put you off your food!

Callery pear

The Callery pear's blossoms may look pretty, but they smell like rotting fish. Ew!

Western skunk cabbage

As the name suggests, this plant smells like a stinky skunk!

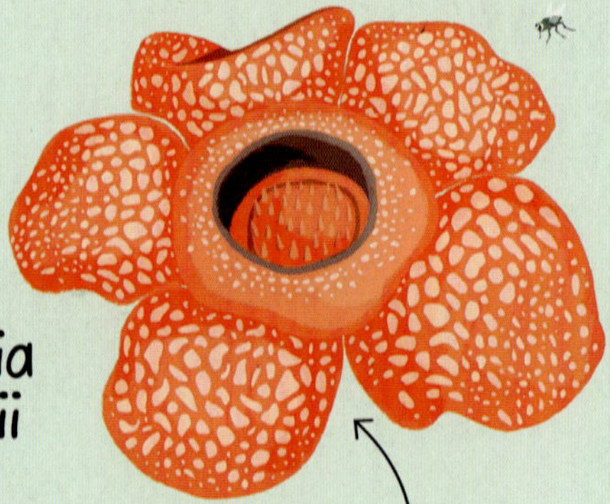

Rafflesia arnoldii

Corpse flowers

These two flowers have both been given the nickname "corpse flower", because they both smell like rotting flesh. The smell attracts flies and beetles. They are two of the biggest flowers in the world.

Hydnora africana

This strange-looking plant smells like poop, which is useful if you want to attract dung beetles.

Titan arum

Cherry pie

This pretty purple flower smells like cherries and vanilla.

Caramel tree

This tree smells like caramel or cotton candy.

Chocolate cosmos

These flowers smell like chocolate. Yum!

Popcorn cassia

This plant smells like buttered popcorn.

Meat-eating Plants

Plants and insects are usually good friends, but some plants catch and eat bugs!

Venus flytrap

Venus flytraps eat almost any small bug! They have leaves that look like little mouths.

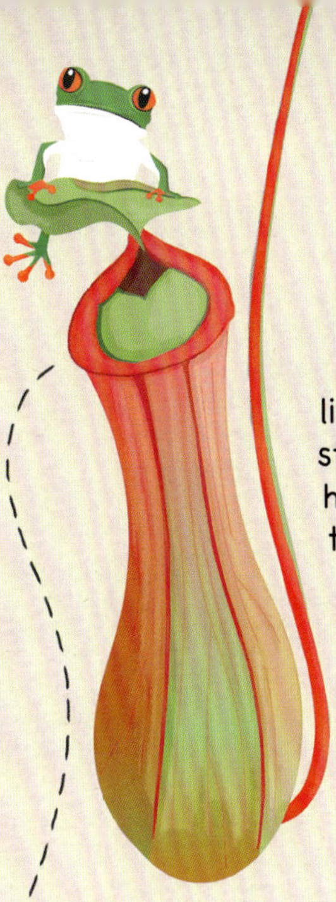

Tropical pitcher plant

Pitcher plants have leaves shaped like jugs. Insects that fall inside get stuck there. Some sneaky tree frogs hang out in or around pitcher plants to catch the flies that they attract.

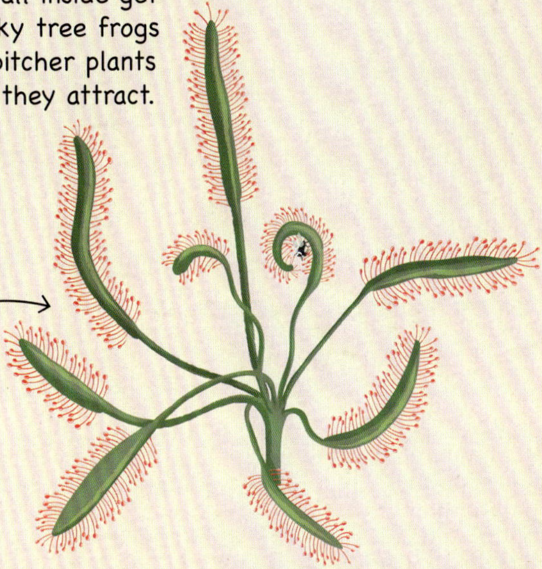

Cape sundew

This plant has tentacle-like leaves, covered in drops of sticky liquid. The plant rolls up its leaves around insects that get stuck.

Trumpet pitchers

This is another kind of pitcher plant that grows long tubes out of the ground to trap insects.

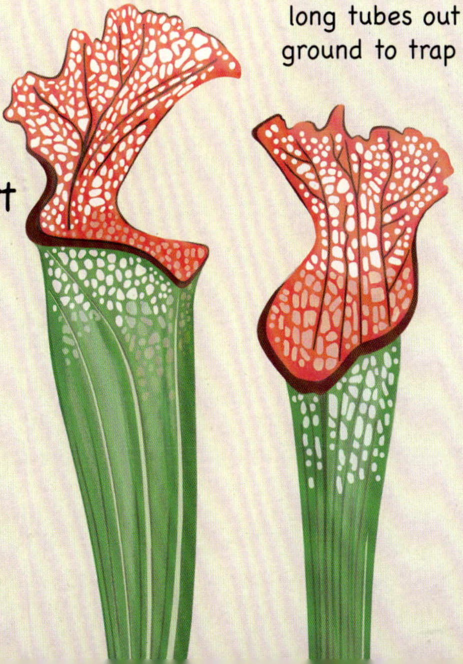

Common butterwort

This flower attracts insects to its sticky leaves, where they get stuck – like flypaper.

Is It a Plant?

There are lots of weird and wonderful-looking plants. Some of them don't look like plants at all! Which disguise do you think is the best?

Hot lips

This rainforest plant has leaves that look like a pouty pair of lips.

Lobster claws

A tropical plant with hanging flowers that look just like lobster pincers.

Bee orchid

This look-alike flower even smells like a bee! It's trying to confuse real bees into pollinating them.

White egret orchid

An amazing flower that looks like a white bird in flight.

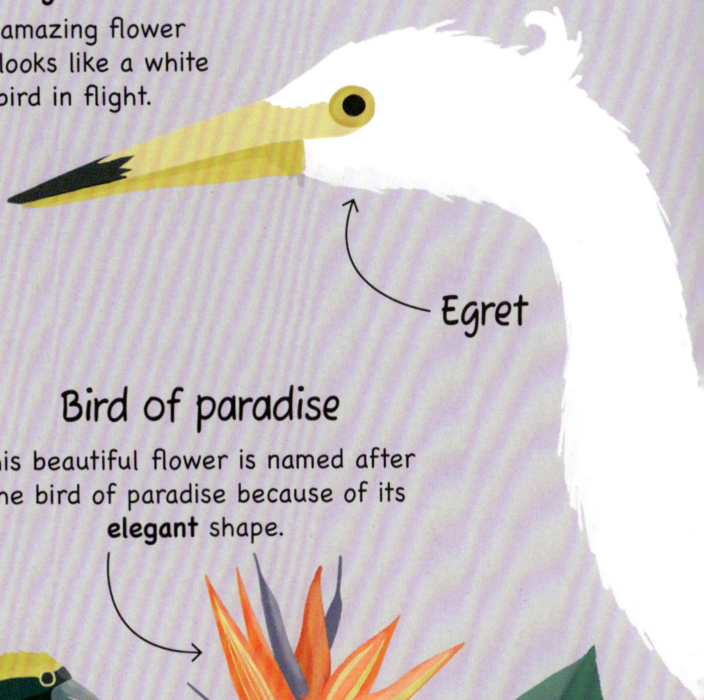

Egret

Bird of paradise

This beautiful flower is named after the bird of paradise because of its **elegant** shape.

Bird of paradise

Lithops

These strange-looking plants are often called "living stones" because they look similar to pebbles on the ground.

Mighty Moss

Moss is amazing! Mosses are small plants that grow in clumps. Sometimes, they spread out covering large areas, like grass. Mosses like damp, shady places, but will grow on almost anything, including trees, rocks and buildings.

Mini forest

Moss is home to many **microscopic** creatures, including "water bears" (tardigrades).

Tallest moss

Not all mosses are small. Dawsonia superba is the tallest moss in the world, and can grow up to 24 inches (61cm) high.

Red sphagnum

Moss isn't always green.

Glowing moss

One moss, sometimes called goblin gold, seems to glow in dark places.

Dung moss

Some moss likes to grow out of animal poop! Yuck!

Let's Make a Moss Jar!

You will need:

- Moss
- Mixing bowl or large container
- Glass jar with lid
- Pebbles
- Soil
- Wood/twigs and stones to decorate
- Figurines/toys to decorate

If collecting moss outdoors, always ask permission, only take small amounts, and collect from areas where there is lots of moss.

1. Soak your moss in a bowl of water for 15 minutes.

2. Add a layer of pebbles to the bottom of your jar. Then add a layer of soil on top.

3. Arrange pieces of wood/twigs and stones.

4. Drain excess water from your moss, then place it on top of the soil, wood, and stones.

5. Add toys and put the lid on your jar. Place it somewhere indoors where it will get some sunlight, but not too much.

Prize Plants

Our big, wide world is home to many extraordinary plants with fascinating features and clever characteristics. There are so many to celebrate, including these prize plants that really stand out from the crowd.

Small but many

The wolffia globosa is the smallest flowering plant in the world! It grows in its thousands and can be found floating on the surface of many **aquatic** habitats, such as ponds and lakes.

It's also known as Asian watermeal and duckweed.

It's a plant with no leaves, stem or roots!

It makes very nutritious meals and is often used in Thai recipes.

Beautifully crafted

The art of creating miniature trees, like bonsai trees, originated in ancient China over 1,300 years ago. The artistic craft came from trimming the trees and training them to grow in beautiful shapes.

It takes about 10 years for a seed to grow into a bonsai tree with wow factor.

This mini plant needs to be looked after every day. They need plenty of water and sunlight but can grow indoors or outdoors.

A bonsai tree that is well-cared for can live to be over 100 years old!

A unique way of growing

The peanut plant grows in an unusual way. The flower petals on the plant drop off, leaving a small growth called a "peg". This bends down and buries itself into the soil. The peanuts grow from the "peg".

Peanuts are sometimes called monkey nuts because they were once a popular food for monkeys in zoos.

This plant loves to grow in a warm and tropical climate.

This delicious snack grows in a pod underground, so needs to be dug up and split open.

Peanut plant pegs

The process from planting to harvesting takes about 4-5 months.

Watch it move!

One special plant species moves so fast that it has been called "dancing plant". They are one of the few plants whose movements are fast enough to be seen by humans.

Shh... if you're quiet around them, you can hear the leaves rustle as they move!

It moves its leaves to catch the sun's light and warmth.

This is a tropical Asian shrub which belongs to the same family as the pea.

Did You Know?

Plants are pretty amazing! Every living creature needs plants to survive; the world wouldn't be the way it is today if we didn't have them. Did you know these amazing facts about plants?

Bamboo is the fastest growing "wood" plant in the world. It grows

35 inches (89cm)

every day!

Pandas eat mostly stems, shoots, leaves, and BAMBOO!

In the 1600s in Holland (The Netherlands), tulip **bulbs** were more expensive than gold!

Seagrass is helping to stop **climate change** by taking in and storing huge amounts of carbon.

Scientists have discovered more than **600** different types of meat-eating plants.

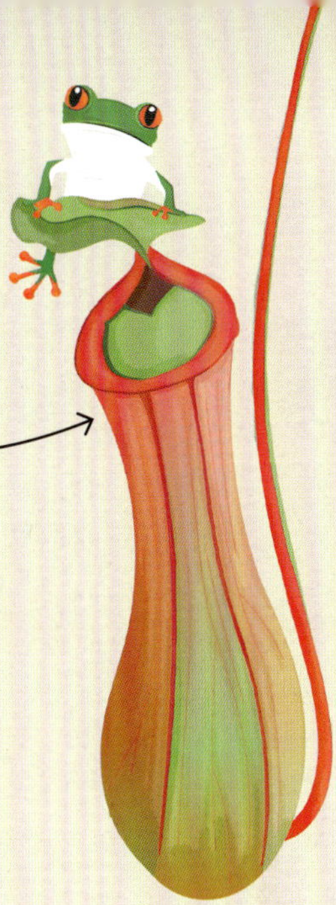

Nepenthes rajah

The Nepenthes rajah stems can grow to nearly **5 feet (1.5m)** tall. It's the biggest meat-eating plant in the world. It's nearly as tall as a brown bear!

The biggest **carnivorous** plants are big enough to trap and eat rats!

The corpse flower, Rafflesia arnoldii, is the biggest flower in the world. It can grow up to **3 feet (1m)** wide!

Match Up the Pairs

Can you match up the fact boxes (below) with the correct plant (right)? Flip back through the book if you need a hint!

1.

I'm a huge red flower which smells like rotting flesh. Ew!

2.

I look like a bird, but I'm actually a tropical flower!

3.

I'm the largest (overall) tree in the world! I am more than 2,200 years old!

4.

I'm a tree which has been around since the time of the dinosaurs! My leaves look like ferns.

5.

I'm a green plant which grows on trees, rocks, and even buildings!

6.

I'm a meat-eating plant. I trap and eat bugs with my mouth-shaped leaves.

General Sherman tree

Moss

Bird of paradise flower

Cycad tree

Rafflesia flower

Venus flytrap

Have you matched them all?

Answers can be found on page 24.

Glossary

Aquatic – something that grows, lives, or spends a lot of time in water.

Bulbs – rounded parts of some plants that grow in the soil. They store food and shoots grow out of them.

Carnivore (carnivorous) – a plant that is able to trap and eat insects and small animals. Also known as meat-eating plants.

Climate change – long-term changes in temperature and weather.

Digest – (verb) to break down food into substances that can be absorbed and used by a body or plant.

Elegant – something that is graceful and stylish in appearance.

Living fossils – a type of plant or animal that has survived for a very long time with very little physical change, and is still around today.

Microscopic – something that is too small to be seen without the use of a microscope.

Nutrients – substances or ingredients that plants and animals need to live and grow.

Pollinate – (verb) when pollen is moved from one plant to another – often by an insect – so the plants can make new seeds.

Seedlings – a young plant, grown from a seed.

Spores – seed-like cells that some living things, including mosses and ferns, use to reproduce.

Trunk – the large woody stem of a tree, where the branches grow from.

Answers to Match Up the Pairs

Answers: 1. Rafflesia flower, 2. Bird of paradise flower, 3. General Sherman tree, 4. Cycad tree, 5. Moss, 6. Venus flytrap.